The Insomniac Liar of Topo

BOOKS BY NORMAN DUBIE

The Horsehair Sofa

Alehouse Sonnets

Prayers of the North American Martyrs

Indian Summer

Popham of the New Song

In the Dead of the Night

The Illustrations

A Thousand Little Things

The City of the Olesha Fruit

Odalisque in White

The Everlastings

The Window in the Field

Selected and New Poems

The Springhouse

Groom Falconer

Radio Sky

The Clouds of Magellan

The Funeral

The Amulet

The Mercy Seat: Collected & New Poems, 1967–2001

Ordinary Mornings of a Coliseum

Untitled Najaf

The Insomniac Liar of Topo

NORMAN DUBIE

The Insomniac Liar of Topo

Copper Canyon Press
Port Townsend, Washington

Copper Canyon Press is in residence at Fort Worden State Park in
Port Townsend, Washington, under the auspices of Centrum, a
gathering place for artists and creative thinkers from around the world,
students of all ages and backgrounds, and audiences seeking
extraordinary cultural enrichment.

LIBRARY OF CONGRESS CATALOGING-IN-PUBLICATION DATA

Dubie, Norman, 1945–
The Insomniac Liar of Topo / Norman Dubie.
p. cm.
ISBN 978-1-55659-263-8 (pbk.: alk. paper)
I. Title.
PS3554.U255I57   2007
811'.54 — dc22
2007013621

3 5 7 9 8 6 4 2
FIRST PRINTING

COPPER CANYON PRESS
Post Office Box 271
Port Townsend, Washington 98368
www.coppercanyonpress.org

for Kaya

ACKNOWLEDGMENTS

The American Poetry Review: "Winter Rains off Pointe du Hoc," "A Gritty Motion Picture Valentine, Denver, 1929," "The Calamitous Dress Harlequin," "At Sunset," "Brahma," "The Last Gold Raptors of Soma," "The Sentimentalists," "Sky Harbor," "George Herbert," "Poem in Praise of the Pacifist Abigail"

Bat City Review: "The Ocean," "Curfew"

Botteghe Oscure: "For My Friend Sush Quintero, Who Brought Me a Book," "On a Low Almond-shaped Mesa," "Epithalamium"

42opus: "Elegy for Robert Creeley," "Tulku"

Gulf Coast: "Elegy"

Interim: "The Hartford V.A.," "Two Stanzas for Timothy Deshaies," "The City of Snow"

Lake Effect: "A Far Horse," "Goya"

Maverick Magazine (online, www.maverickmagazine.com): "Election Night," "The Bills of Mortality"

Ploughshares: "The Insomniac Liar of Topo," "The Idea of Soup"

Poetry Northwest: "A Practical Song of Two," "On the Ordination of a Zen Monk"

Poets & Writers (online, www.pw.org): "The Wolf's Lair," "The Coroner's Confession," "The Kites of Shrove Monday," "Out of the Mouth of Cygnus"

Romantic Circles Praxis: "The Tantric Master, Lord Marpa, Twice Dreamt of the Prophet, William Blake"

Runes: "Plover Field '43"

West Town Press (St. Louis): *Untitled Najaf* (a chapbook): "Untitled Najaf," "Storm," "A Black Madonna…," "Winter Notes of an Old Chinese Bureaucrat"

"Encanto's Ferry" was accidentally eliminated from my collected poems and is now included here.

"George Herbert" is for my daughter, Hannah.

The poem "Elegy" is secretly for David Gilmore.

At the conclusion of "Sky Harbor," admiration for H.H., the 16th Karmapa.

The title poem for this volume has for its subject the life of the Italian filmmaker Federico Fellini.

A special gratitude to my friend Chris Burawa for all his attention, support, and fine work.

—N.E.D.

Contents

The Insomniac Liar of Topo

I

Head of hair smelling like
the tuberose and triumphant entry
into Rome…

SARAH VAP

The Wolf's Lair

The swarming deerflies carry a bloom of narcissus
to the bench in the chapel's loft
where the priest lay in putrefaction
from Monday to this Saturday's supper.

The exorcists growing disconsolate
in their birchpaper hats
went down to the ruins by the river
with buckets of ale and scalded eels.

The peach sacks of the mad women of Oilliers
flew from the mountain
to the grim winter wood, where
like comets drunken with millennia
they shot through the illustrated shadows
of dead S.S. and their cannon mules—
the wood smoldering through Lent.

There were fireflies inside the houses of the rich.

(Illustrated with what, the phosphor
of cadaver and a poor potato farmer's
bag of lime.
Anyone who slept at night was sick throughout the morning.)

Margaret rested her head on the cork floor
of the Führer's walk-in freezer.
I struck my head with a stone
to stop the birdsong.
Then together we ate bark off the willow.

Just last year the Führer was nervous
about his back-acre in the mountains—
how deer from nowhere clattered into the meadow
to the minefields—there was a thunderclap—
and generals with their women stepped into the garden
where the rose mist painted the stunned deer
diagonally before the green sun. One
of the bearded stags standing on three legs.
Martin Bormann shot him nicely in the chest
with just a gold-plated pistol. The creature
fell over and another geyser of venison
rained down around us.
The Führer said a good afternoon was had by all—
and that the animals' empty expressions
betrayed to him the laughter of Mother Nature.

Plover Field '43

for Kristi

Rowing, last Monday, after the air raid:
sudden fields of lightning
made an electric sand shark
out of the blasted bridge—the revolving
cattle guard gone blue and orange with teeth—
just vast bottom locking,
and frenzied skids of tail,
a sprung hubcap off the keeper's Pontiac
taken for the fish's angry eye—
the giant squids were more dark cable
falling everywhere with the hail.

The saliva of sea creatures was
in our hair.
Helen, with the Lord's help,
said a crow flew past
like a woman's scalp. The cooks laughed.

I wished I was back in "the cactus Tuileries"
in old Tucson.
All I could think of was Mother's
mesquite line running past gophertown
to the artesian pond
with its woodbox and windmill.

A wave slaps my breasts and neck: between waves
airy escalators of kelp
are crashing around us.
We took the red-eye to Bellingham.

The plane's propellers were faint multiplying
flowers in a pollen cloud of pink exhaust—   dragging

like lost Mormon strophes
across a cotton rag of paper.
The rusted box plane lifted
over scattering sheep, the dry arroyo
for an ax handle.
This is how Helen and I went to war—
dry, with our boots on, smelling of glory
and lye soap.

The Hartford V.A.

August 4, 1967

While the night fell across the hospital lawn
we watched a red squirrel attack a kite
that was lifting off a stone bench.
It burst through the paper and sticks
like a trained lion through hoops of fire.
The discouraged orderly
tossed aside his cigarette, tossed
his large white ball of string
at the dark window where Nurse Mallet
and I were trying not to laugh,
my stitches dry across my stomach.

Mallet yelling,
"Jim, did you teach that animal
to do that?" He gave
her the middle finger
and the gunnery sergeant
across from us, arm and leg raised high
in plasters, vomited
blood across Mallet's white nylons.

He apologized five or six times
and died just as the sun was rising,
climbing through itself, a small
diamond of fire, paper
and sticks, cheap paste and ribbons
of significance.

Two Stanzas for Timothy Deshaies

The lit windows of the train rise
against the night field
with women and children sacking beets
in a near-freezing rain; a little girl with fever
believes that coffins of light
are shooting past them
on a high parallel to the shadow
of a ruined aqueduct
and an equally ruined constellation, *ursa major*.

The red-haired woman
turns the horse toward the house and barn.
Later that night
she'll smile crawling into the bed
with her twin brother and small sister. Red
heated stones in with them.
Snow now falling from the sky
into the open rivers of their arms and legs.

Someone snoring out behind the mountains.

You said to us that you never
quarreled with your wife. Good night.
Tim Deshaies. Good night.

The Coroner's Confession

The chokeberry folds into the dead grasses.
The late frost leaping
among a stark cribbage of geraniums —
a blade of ice fell here
from the culvert in the night.

My wife is in Gallup
until the second Friday in Lent...
Her mother's burial. And
an arthritic spaniel
who must be put down.

All night the deer were in the trees
mewing for salt. Finally,

with a red tablecloth
I ran out after them.

The screen door
startled instead the peacocks on the shed.
The violet eyes on their fans woke me
screaming. I'll be glad

of my wife's return.
And of an exchange of seasons.

Winter Rains off Pointe du Hoc

in memory of Alan Dugan

The wind is a failure of forms,
a calamity of content—it is
cutting the white peaks from great
green waves
making cold abbreviations of salt
that are the pith eyes on ghosts.

Across the cliffs
in the fields above the water
martyred dead rest in some soft
tropic of wind, some tropic of the hidden variable

that pierces sinew, neck,
or the helmet. The suits
praise his valor, the gunnery sergeant Nash
from Missoula, Montana, who says
the bear nests up in the wind
with a smile of margarine,
has courage, and
the bear is my friend —

when the bear stumbles,
you ba-bas must understand,
the bear dies large
not like a pigeon at a Legionnaires Convention.

Elegy for Robert Creeley

The sun broke through…

I read aloud on the balcony
your poem for the "two wives,"

a finch flew
through the ice shavings
of the sprinkler system

to my railing— it bowed deeply
twice
in gratitude
for what you had written

is my best explanation?

The Insomniac Liar of Topo

Snow like the cold lard of falling stars
strikes the windshield.
A small thermos of tea
rolls around in the glove compartment.

I sneeze.

Up in the black trees, the moon
and the snow are repeatable
in the long spine of a woman
who has opened her high window.

It is her signal
to the idiot spatio-cosmocrat
sucking on a toothpick
at the foot of the yellow orchard ladder.

The ladder rises through cloud
with the simple valor
of a shadowy niche
where the heart of a lamp burns,
not cleanly.
Not cleanly.

The old one who is counting the coins
was a champion swimmer from Madrid.
Her winters are passed
guarding this rough pine closet
that is an entrance for the turnpike
to the North.
The stove burns a red kerosene.

Let's not get involved –

the darker cloud has devoured
the cosmocrat's shoes and suspenders.
The woman's spine is now draped in a bright sheet

and she lifts from the window
into the rose light of the hills,
which are, like her,
also sailing into the disturbed limitless waters

of a winter orchard.

Storm

Lightning in the trees. Hail bounces
on the neighbor's clay roof.
I have overslept. I remember
what it was like living with people.

Tulku

the letter of discovery

It is both the depth of field and snow
that have shortened the telephone poles
by half or more.

The yellow flower boxes below the windows
are desultory with graying pea-strings.

The many-storied intersection
of river, limestone tunnel, and railbed
stand back from the birches
and collapsing roadhouse.

(Out of rime,
here, is his birthplace —   this next time —
three miles from the Pennsylvania state line.)

He's the talented forward of a red blouse
and broken arc of gravity's javelin
rattling loudly inside the empty high-school bleachers.

Hot chocolate, cheese sandwiches roasted
in seconds on a coal pan
inside the open furnace.

The girl Eileen for a mother,
she, looking into the fire-horse year
for a father, sees her brother
that June leaping sun share,
sylph share, into the cold emerald waters
of the abandoned quarry. William

with goldenrod for certificates
of birth and marriage.
William and the sudden rain
making a plenitude,
nipples rising across the surface of water.

A pale hip rolls up from the depth,
the floating hairline touches the quarry's lip.

The City of Snow

for Jim

These are dry bellicose men
who charge across a field like red violins,
like chariots framed in cedar
by a highly mathematical Egyptian magus.

Elementary, that the Lord made us
in his image, so that by the very end of days
he would recognize uncannily
himself in the lumber of Charlie McCarthy.

This is my poem for a man who's dead
at his own hand.
Dead, blamelessly, if you were to ask.

No doubt, deep within Mississippi
there's a sister
and a tree. White mules
are dragging a box through rhubarb. The testament

is in Greek, it witnesses
Enos Slaughter rising above a summer's runner—
a baseball diamond
where the chalk lines
have been erased by large men
throwing themselves against bags of sand.

It's wrong to think that you are dead
just because another lives;
conversely, vote, if you wish

the other stained thumb of a Spring Offensive
in a far desert city
with unlimited sand so hot, in fact,
it impugns the child's brow like falling snow itself.

The Kites of Shrove Monday

There was a clattering of dishes. Our Muslim visitors
walked into the still standing
gray field of sunflowers.
Each visitor with a square spool of waxed string.
Beyond the field
there was the burnt egg of the abandoned monastery,
and then the sea's cliff. The visitors
were never heard from again.
I wasn't even nine when what didn't happen
happened yet again…

Untitled Najaf

Some black abstract honey of isinglass
cracks like giant wooden fans
where a sudden desert wind lifts—
sweeping their wings
into even more violent advantages
among the thousands of tombs,
beside a mosque, across dry land to the horizon.

A white or gold light at the foot of ladders
that are toppling
in the night while hand to hand
they fight, Marines in soot-shine
and the tattered militias, their baffled blood
stinks on the dark shellac of ground.

Under the interrupted stars
the darker, even larger, wings
of wool and feather-paste shift to rotate
at the rabbit-bone
joint centered in the shoulder blades—
fallen nudes in a moody crystal ledge
of air. Here, time itself boxes them
in its fast glassy luggage of octahedron.

Here, everywhere, are the nickel wells of relay,
dead birds, and a purple horsehair ottoman
burning now these past seven days.

A Black Madonna Visits the Tombs of the Sacred Crocodiles; *circa XII Dynasty.*

> The Magdalen nuns saw their original mission as
> the salvation of prostitutes. In time, however, that
> definition was expanded to include young women
> guilty only of loving a man of their choice before
> they were married.
>
> MARY ANN SORRENTINO

I

Outside the smokehouse,
under the blue-gray moon of the Hill
she culls string beans
while stressing that this sack
of deer bones
has absolutely nothing to do
with her being the mother of Sergeant-major;
that that she's dreaming
of the out-there, somewhere:

       where in greasy greenish shalebed
the blacker *that-that* dogs
unearthed the skeleton of a woman
with red and white string threading
her spinal column— it seems to be
nearly marbled with decomposition,
               tattooed
three-dimensionally with lichen?

Her son said
long wind-stars illustrated
all her joints as if with diamonds. The corpse

didn't want fat at the tannery
of her hinges, making a metaphor of jewels
for badly educated boys from Cambridge
who are digging in her evening landscape —
this goes, also, for Sergeant-major. Most of all him?
Lef — tenant, lef-tenant, now *him.*

Well, from the looks of things
the dogs found mice nesting in the pelvis,
infant socks, they said,
some cleft but still sucking mud.

It will always go hard on a woman.
And with a hood

of bleached cotton she looked straight into her. And saw both
American and Arab girls dying there
in a weird childbirth of living rock.

What could this possibly mean? Say, for
Sergeant-major — is he still smiling
under a night's confetti
for a gang of one.
Poor chub in a tub of cubed ice in Samadine —

the channel nearly frozen
the winter of her crossing —
like Washington
on the prow of a riverboat, this Magdalene
walks across the Christmas pudding…

In flying machines,
the Brits —   in the air, bombing a watercolorist's
version of serene Iraqi villages —
wanting the crosshairs to be perfect

for the smart baby Bombardier. He's getting
it right, between two World Wars, in the great dynasty

of the crocodile emerging between two bushes, beyond
the long linen piers.

II

These brother kings, 'zziah and 'zekiah, sit on donkey skulls
in the cruel rains of a winter desert.

You must think this a lamentation
for the burned children in their distant villages. The way
all their mouths are open.

I'm sorry, but our sacred necessities,
the brother kings, are
just having a noon meal of seed packets
and pinkish owl brains.
Their high priest fills

a horse's bladder with white rainwater
from the eaves of red rock
naturally sledged by strong winds
and a loose gully-rough of thistle, agate
clutch, and all that dead cactus

draped in purple pinstriped pajamas. You can bury the late
Latin lesson in plurals past the agave
with the snake fossil, all late-American theatricals, or
UPI—Moscow—

"there are UFOs over Turkey!"
And earthquakes
have formed a sinkhole nearly

the size of Tehran (*well, a
throat-clearing*), in Tehran.

The narrowing blue feet

of a woman pass just under his vision.
The Scribe sighing, *sister catherine, sister catherine.*
Then more of the shuffling of blue feet across Mount Sinai…

III

So, the high priest, Mythic Destraktus, is now drinking
the pod-water of immortality again.

He boils the spineless button succulents
of a chequered red and yellow mantle
while tossing in a pearled-belly slake of mad
Egyptian frog.

This is when the bound blue feet of the levitating
Magdalene
tramp below the sun visors of Moses
and the Elders. Flak-jacketed
Moses Destraktus never shared with us
this little foible of the alien mountain god, she
being a Goddess,
                    and strapped, at *that-that…*

IV

The priest says to his brother kings
that the horse bladder
is still filling with waters
to enable

a tolerance for a dimension of future knowledge
that will burst ALL

while disturbing none. Yes, the Mother-
Sergeant-major is in the bloodline
of Magdalene leaving the fog of the hillside garden.

Bloodsucking little vudjras
fanning us with fronds and matchsticks, little lariats
from the paste-pot filling the air—   a great one,
Archangel Uriel, pointing at the beloved servant, crying
imposter, recent monster, *journaliste mort*, witch

of Alexandria,

      v

feeble starlight of things past, fat
spawn of glass and herself! But when
did she suffer more
or less? Her raised torch

with its trailing smudge or banner of fruit bats
just sprung from the Egyptian labyrinths,
Lion & Lamb. The short sequence
of fireworks like a scribbling of vipers
in your coal dark hair. In this current delirium
trying to trade a plum Studebaker convertible, *friend*,
for a barge of gold
she intervenes, "...*did you say something, louder, please;*
          Satan's dogs are
ripping me from living English rock." She

thought she heard the prayer of a legless man
            crawling out of a cold desert depot...

VI

Above them, the saw-toothed moons and wind
eat all night
the pack mules falling from the hillsides.

But just above us
in Iranian airspace
the gold disks
leapt past the brightening palms.
They lifted water from the mountain lake, sheet lightning
now general across Siberia.

The man with no legs, who prayed for death
that long night in a circle of his own blood, now
is opening his newsstand—   clean Egyptian bread
in his hands. His dog-god

eats old rice and the leg and shoulder of a rat
out of a surviving brass cymbal, the other
lost to the winter quake—
along with his two daughters
who just this year
began to walk with their instruments
in the holiday bands. A saint day,

the green and yellow mosque
burning during the worst
of the aftershocks. What he feels
for his dead daughters
is what he feels for the lost legs.

He feels shame
with all the inscribable nervous ailments
of ghosts. He hides his pain

in the greasy immeasurable ink of headlines.
There's suffering for you!

Like an incandescent reed —
an American flag burns in his brain.

VII

The still-living Sergeant-major,
up from Basra,
with chain valise and sidearms, speaks
irritably to the legless shopkeeper
who'd like to seal up
some lost gospel within Sergeant-major's chest cavity —
just a baseball stitch, amber flypaper,
and the paraffin…

Yet in a broken spirit, instead,
he says,

take right and two lefts,
bank is there
with billboard of winter. Two smokestack,
and water plants

(not irises, Sergeant-major thinks),
without bliss.

Addam before eating the river grasses
found the gates of Ishtar
and swept the porch of cats and balancing pans —

his daughter read French verse to him,
some aesthetic of innocence and sickness
burning with the stench

of green cigars. *Baudelaire's ghost giving a ragged*
middle finger to the Suez Canal.

This moment is not their Communion either.

It's clear to me they're all innocent—
I can't really separate them in this sunlight.

The ones who are shirtless and rowing in the boats
under the flaming howitzer pigeons—*now,*
are they the jackals? Pass the instructions
to the rear please. The legless veteran

of two desert wars is now grooming his dog, an unreachable spot.
At the neck, with his teeth searingly,

                                    "dearie, you are all savages,

save me," he thinks.

VIII

And the black shadow in the dead khaki fronds
is just the gentle movement of a flag. The smell of a niece.
The mowed lawns
and burning cars. His passport photo
shows Sergeant-major thinning
in the coastal air, the mother and sister

IX

are gathering for his burial.
Where has their hair gone. *Under a cloth to the ground,*
out of the German
birdcage—it was like golf balls
exploding across the canal, and the cars
burning for miles.

The sun drooping into the laps of streetlamps, a passing
limousine filled with sailors, their blouses
just now bloodied;
they scream while laughing.
They say millions of birds are settling in Marseilles.

I lean across the table
to share with Sergeant-major's ghost
a story of the wonderful equivocal sailor—

but Sergeant-major is chewing his ice,
he swallows,
saying, "Sir, if you see me Mum, will ya tell her
I'm dead. Like a doorknob." He laughs.
I did see a whore once in Marseilles

translated into clouds. Hand grenades taped to red and yellow cans of petrol.
A jellyroll of fertilizer.
Like a doorknob.

    I saw one do it once, I mean with a brass doorknob,
    white paint splattered all over it and the door—

    whatcha do is
    stand on the tippy-toes of the left leg, the other leg
    folds and rises into the right armpit,
    the left arm points
    upwards nearly to the open transom,
    the right hand on the right breast,
    the left knee drops, not even a centimeter,
    and the abdomen is sucked up
    —saliva inching
    down the door—at this moment, her best friend,
    also nearly naked, bursts
    into the room. There was what I took

for an enviable groan (just when the buttocks
smacked the florets of the wallpaper).
Laughing. Done flying. She gathers

herself up and with the red glass slipper
begins to put out the eyes of her friend. *I am now*

exaggerating. Though, it was just then that the petrol bombs
went off. I thought,
I am Marlene Dietrich, buried alive in beach sand.
Don't tell the Mum anything. Mum with one lung collapsed—

he smiles.
She never had much fun. She never did understand us.

II

Winter Notes of an Old Chinese Bureaucrat:

A rope was tossed over a white branch—

oxen moving through deep snow,

the smoke from their manure
combined to encircle the thief in his skirt
who was suddenly conveyed by oxen into air,
his feet seemingly kicking
free of perfect wreaths of ammonia—
farther dispersed, they could be seen
broken, moving past a day moon

into the coastal province of my birth.

Out of the Mouth of Cygnus

First the dogs go missing. Then the days.
It was an aftershock in the first week,
a sudden scum of movement
alive with stunned mosquitoes
over all the swimming pools
east of the great alkali deserts.
Just that least observable movement —
a breath of chlorine —
with the loud dark wings of flies
lifting in a cloud to eye level. Then, again,

the long coastal land becoming
a rope bridge over an unlikely void
with a meridian best described by the blind.
The phantom pendulum that arouses
an average value —   the line
from groin to the morphine heaps of the mind.

The halved illustrated doll houses
with sleepwalkers standing in the archways,
mostly naked; so fixed
that the plumber on the third floor
looks a victim of crucifixion.

I believe William James dreamt
of the San Francisco quake
and yet arrived in time to experience it
because of a long-standing
speaking commitment
that he could not, in all honor, abdicate.

We have not yet guessed
at a 21st-century gentleman, author or mystic,
with his manners and engagements,
no burden of harmonics or imagination, just screaming—
running mad across some draining lake
way beyond the city limits:

He's kneeling now in a rose excitement of wings,
of blond fleas, and James would have noted
in his journal that they
would eat him clear to the bone, with the sinew snapping
like violin strings.

Encanto's Ferry

He left the tent of the soup kitchen, passing
a friend without speaking. A mockingbird
freeing every song it had heard
in those last brackish hours of evening.
He lit a cigarette. Something clean
like gin was what he was missing...

He walked over the gravel to the new power station,
which at night is like a chandelier
of guttering, blank candles. He threw burlap
over the barbed wire
and dropped into a shallow security pond.
He climbed the ladder of the smokestack, turning
his back to it, facing the wind —

spread-eagle, he dove, falling in silence
into the cat's cradle of live wires, discrete
moth-sear and sage in the desert air —
the neighborhoods went black in every direction.

A 707 was coming in along the dry riverbed.
A passenger, looking down on the spreading darkness,
saw at the center of it   a suspended
human form on fire.
She folded her hands and buried them
in the crotch of a purple dress, vomiting

onto the bald head of the man seated in front of her.
She said, much later, "He must have been disturbed?"
The wheels of the plane now touching the earth.
In our words,
power was being restored to the suburbs.

A Gritty Motion Picture Valentine, Denver, 1929

for L.J.

The tree bloomed forward into a dark snow
without an accumulation like simple coins
or data.
Nevertheless, this April night, snowplows
scraped the road of salt— each a strongbox
with a single chain sparking the long winter
into a bleak surmise of sunrise,
which is, of course, both fire
and fire's aggrandizement
like talcum on a round of mirror glass.

In the early light we must kill William Blake
while first accusing him: Sir,

what do you know of bloodthirsty Cree playing
lacrosse with purple cabbages, acorn squash? Did you
take my mother to the theater last night
and later have your way with her? More cabbages?

Did you travel here in a war canoe of birth
made sleek with the fat of opossum?

There was some interval between questions
marked by silence: by his offering

a bowl with tobacco smoke in it.
It was then he slipped a knife into your trouser knee
that he might take flight. *Guitars rising.*
And you say, I really

now must leave this dream. One way please. One way.
But I'll be the one to make these decisions.
And you are fully awake. *Toot-toot.*

Blood leaving the vessel, lacy, for the boot.

The Ocean

after Hjalmarsson

She woke, I think, while demonstrating for me
the rain-soaked grandmother
pushing a green roll-away bed
over the sea cliff.
Where she found this privilege
of childhood,
I cannot guess.
In that last warm beer maybe, I said,
lighting her cigarette and breasts.

The Calamitous Dress Harlequin

They say she withstood the green light of orchard limes
in Andromeda.
The mi-shuttlecock so hot approaching the mother ship
that all eighteen eyeballs in sleeper berths
baked hard like plover eggs in the Pullman car
while descending into endless prairie grasses.

Skinned buffalo climbing the horizon like hives.
The smell reached them before they could confirm
that moonlight was slicing at the white-fatted haunches
in the manner of a wanton crime.

Grated basil and old Parmesan on the edges of the corn muffins.
Hot berries draped over venison.
The coffee with crushed eggshells and pebbles from a stream
in Colorado.

They ate with large knives and forks backward.
One man from Maine spit a whole slew of tomato seeds
across the ceiling. The "bone man"
from Johns Hopkins University said it was a map of the night sky
and pointing toward some unchewed corn
beyond the reddening array of seeds, said

Damn it all if she didn't survive
that fireball in Andromeda
and then last night with the benefit of her big boot
pulls that black tooth from a pitiable circus grizzly
she subdued with just her bare loins
and half a barrel of amber whiskey.

Elegy

Listening to the children while growing cold
on the beach—
something on the black shellac radio
about a hurricane crossing Cuba.

Think of inflating balloons
and a yellow birthday cake
with a mule fly shocked
and dying in equal parts
of sugar and paraffin whisked
into a troubled sea of egg whites
and berries gathered by the children
on the hill this morning.

The brother said to his sister
you idiot
bring the colander here
this minute
before I spill them.

The desert city
falling away from its own noise.

I look out over the coal barge
while listening to the green waves
eating away at the road's
unlikely culvert. It is these minimal
doglike irises
that are our vindication.

They'll stand in a blue bottle
next to the cake—   while
the drunk uncle fingers them
singing "Happy Birthday"
to Arafat. He's blotto. A ghost
of a man
who actually fell rushing a sniper's nest
in a wet potato field outside Tiberias.

The small boy has mangled
my irises. They are on the sand. And
his sister is collecting flies
in the blue bottle.

The sun is setting.
I look into it and say, "Ishmael,
how could you be dead—
you were still a kid
when I last spoke to you?"

The consequences of saying this are
not negligible—the flowers
strewn everywhere beneath a picnic table.

At Sunset

Fucking get back. I have cut
the white paper gasket
out of the apple. Yes,
it's a seed packet
like the wife's whalebone jacket
ruling the fat lamps of the Orient.
The faint straight lace of it,

sounds.
Ashes and wormwood
in a brand drawer.
The horses' testicles tossed
into straw for the cats.
Was it not mad John Clare—
that night, and it mad, *last night Clare* saying
it was a sound
going off in his head. A mainmast snapping.
The man standing next to you hears it.
Suddenly you're naked running through pasturage
like a woman's hair.

A Far Horse

for Kit

There is an original privacy of mind
that is the pond sealing its sky window
with the sweat jewels of pickerel
and pike
lounging in the autumn night
while laughing at a solitary passing car
with its fickle satellite links
weak beside the sleep
and simple magnitude
of a pond that's realized
its skin of ice,
formed twice, not spontaneous yet healed
beyond a boathouse and its faded box kite.

No pathetic carbon
parenthesis of skunks
from a drizzling April to a drizzling November.
Just this other growth of snow
with a shale-green fishing shack
unused that winter
because of a cancer of the stomach.

The old Ford truck abandoned
on a minor logging road
is an artifact of the father who, ginless,
impresses the sheriff with his version
of that damned bright saucer
flying just above the smoky pine tops—

just more of those aliens
feeling nostalgia for their coldest moon,
trafficking over potato fields;
the sad-asses, breaking dimensions
like flatland pencils,
looking for life again where there is none.

He's still thinking of the tourmaline
pickerel flesh —
his mother cleaning fish out in that squat
kitchen sink
that was the original rattlesnake bassinet
where she washed the mustard shit
off dancing legs
clear in mountain water to his ankles.

So there may be fish guts, lizard men
in the government, and a red-haired surgeon
discarding lengths of his intestine…

but under a new moon
there in the dark hospital room
he suddenly loses all fear,
knows the pond is freezing over
while he swims down among the lilies
where the scum of the long brown rope
stripes his back with light.
He is happier,

happier than those alien Greys
in their titanium crafts of amethyst strobe
getting their kicks flying over
fucking hopeless upstate New York.

Brahma

The news of the poisoned duck spread beyond the household, so the false Gautama, in a small but ancient tradition of men, freshened all the lamenting birds by commanding that their necks be wrung. This is axial to the idea of compassion. Look down from your upper room. This is the doom of supper and white candles.

On the Ordination of a Zen Monk

for Chris

Bashō is boiling his summer robes
beside a pond
with six red trees drowning in it —
his young friend is ripping
sides of flesh
off the steaming white catfish —
his knife still has the juice of apple on it.

Over the hill
court archers are at their new sport
of dog-killing. Bashō has
immersed himself in the pond
but can still hear the peacocks
crying over the one wounded dog
who is running from the hunters
in the azure costumes.

When they find the poor animal
he is eating the earth, grinding his face into it
in an attempt to suffocate.
The archers mock the dog's suffering.

The weak leader in our *heike* senate
with a bad heart
shot a lawyer in the face
in dry standing corn —
there are
bits of white corn on his face
like fragments of human teeth.

The standing corn is a traditional refuge
for scrawny birds. The sleeves of the shocking corn
bleed as well. Bashō cries to these hunters
who will shit rocks in hell
where time has no meaning and dogs
dispense mercy
to government officials and their wives
who also have lived lives that are cruel,

even brutal.

Election Night

A woman inside a black and gold shade
is eating rice with small
red peppers shredded in it. She washes
her face, a large insect
with an arcade pincerlike hand
clawing through silver-plated timepieces,
sunglasses with turquoise lenses and a copper blade
for paring toenails or peaches.

This mind reader is a muse of terrible futures.
This morning she said
that she was not surprised by the pool
of urine on the kitchen tiles.
She did not berate the miniature dog
but rather her husband. He thinks,

while stepping over the waters,
that damn pond where the gray monk
drowned his two kittens. Sleeping
all winter, then the cook's sister
realizing the cold bastard was dead.

A clairvoyant from the suburbs of Detroit,
she whispers to her client
while choking on incense.
Suck it up, dearie. The zipper scar
on your belly is romantic
like an amber centipede dragging itself
across wet rocks in Scottish moonlight.

And Doris left her partial plate
in a water glass
in that new Denny's in Sandusky, Ohio.
George is not sleeping with your cousin Martha.
Neither is she sleeping with him.

She stirs the money in the tray.
A barrette out of place. She changes
dollars over peroxide and paint.
Laxatives and tranks.

She came to the bookstore in the dark, leaves now
in the rain. Whispering
again, this time into the cell,
telling her new lover,
from across town, that she's
a red-haired cashier in an Algerian canteen. Then,

Abbé, Abbé,

she steps into the wet neon and screams—
a stabbing pain to her temple, she smooths,
arranges her blouse
and speaks in her greening voice—   *I know*
the very brand of carpet vacuum
Karl Rove, ten years from now,
will purchase for a summer house
in West Virginia –   *he sits*

drinking a warm Bordeaux in the guilty dark
while the Electrolux's robot saucers and trolley
pass silently through the rooms collecting dirt.
Yes, sweetie, an Electrolux
like some wonderful aqua bus decorated
with diamonds, ashes and citrine rough

literally lifting in the dark and out the window
over the Smokies, Everglades, the brown sea,
then over a retired Manhattan cop who's been diagnosed
with senile dementia – this, their last visit to the Yucatán.

He points up with the other tourists
standing there among claret paper lamps
across the rolling lawns of Palenque –
saying, "I don't believe my eyes, Sondra,
but it looks just like the spaceship that blew up
over Palestine, Texas,
while your brother, below, was taking
his famous dump in poison oak:

he thought it was Russian space junk,
the most beautiful sight in his life, until
later that night when Jill
caked his body in cortisone,
strapping his wrists in gauze to the camper bed
and then force-feeding him Valium
against, as his mother said, all circumstances? God
but he was red."

Karl's robot now negotiating
the plush stairs
is attacked by the fifteen-pound tomcat
called Roosevelt
and that's all they wrote about that boy's toy.
Honey, I gotta go…   like the man said,
"history is progress."

Curfew

We need salt and clean linen?
A moon
is in the landlord's vineyards.
It must be a simple burial
but without fault
we need fresh linen and the salt.

The Idea of Soup:

*after the slaying of eight children at the church wall
of Candelária*

The women would come in Chevrolets
with soup in tins for the children.

The women would come in Chevrolets,

tin within tin, for the children.
The children nearly sleepwalk

in the exhaust. They are lost
dragging their blankets

through the long pepper fog of Chevrolets.

The papers said the dead children
were unwashed.
Not of the blood. I think not. To think
policemen could arrive disguised
as Chevrolets. As soup of the day
from some banquet hall in downtown Rio.

*The rain on the tin –
of the tiny baby Jesus pressed
in tin.*

Soup and big banks are such simple things—

like these dead children
whose mouths are filling,
equally, with soup and the rain.
Rain?

See, they *were* washed
of the blood
of baby Jesus, naked, on pine tables with kerosene.

III

*Then when I add a six-inch stick
and remove the two-inch stick,
the four-inch stick becomes the
shorter one…*

Emptiness is interdependent
origination.

THRANGU RINPOCHE

The Tantric Master, Lord Marpa, Twice Dreamt of the Prophet, William Blake

for Mark

The great translator thought
he had suffered the sleep of a cloudless day
in a boat of skins
on a cold and black inland sea.

Elohim, the eye of minor periphery,
broke bread with him on the moonlit water.
He washed his beard and hair
and said your daughters are now stepping from furnaces.
But if we wake
by their drying looms
with a mountain of salt between me and them,
then the diarist wife
has taken these margins of yellowing shoreline
from us.

London sleeps with its cousins and sisters all winter
while naked surgeons cross through the city
bearing torches...   well, citizens,

this is the cult of worms
who by physical inches of devotion are measuring a churchyard.
The owls forming a morbidly obese quotation
from Ovid.

The Word is always out weeping in the evening
refusing the hot custards, stealing

from sick and defenseless travelers.
The last Republic is out too, burning on the horizon.

Phoenician men sitting on the purple rocks
mending their nets, chewing
on roots, laugh
and then walk out across the water.

They've been doing it for centuries,
that is—   mending their nets with laughter.

The Bills of Mortality

Cádiz due east…   cucumber esters and mustards.
Actually, there were large bronze esters,
virtual vinegars in the skin
of certain rodents. And the fleas avoided them.
During plague in Holland
whole sleeping costumes were made of these rats:

the fat diamond cutter and his wife,
snoring on their bellies, a red candle
guttering beyond them, dream of the dead aunt

who woke to a plague warden in the early morning
nailing shut her doors.
Posting the writ of quarantine after finding the aunt's
husband in the night rounds—   delinquent, cobbled,
his nightshirt torn to the navel
and tulips blooming in his armpits.

The Chinese symbol for discord is two Jesuits
burning in the same wood.
The pope desired spices, sweaty tea of cumin
and the bolting silk…   *Rome*
romanizes Rome.
The yellow charcoal scars the chapel door.

Exeunt. Exeunt. Gobble, gobble.
No more.

II

the document states that my little brother was
dying of a.i.d.s.
                              we went to his rustic cabin,
with the obese lilacs, in pennsylvania—   at that green lake
with the loons & voodoo…   so, to be safe,
before i sat on his toilet seat
i wrapped my johnson twice in toilet paper
& adhesive tape—   so dig, we're riding that trombone
of an old ford to town & john's senile mother
has stuffed my burlesque hat with twenty
dollar bills & hard candy—   it sitting in my lap
& i start screaming that ants are everywhere
& the vehicle comes to a halt, bo diddly on the radio,
while i'm stripping in the headlights, down
to that ragged wasp's nest,

john & andy sweeping red ants like asian horsemen
off my dancing ass, my brother's head resting on the wheel—
he laughs, he cries & is seized while saying that
this is his last triumph. plague & the country life.
that's all that i can remember.

The Last Gold Raptors of Soma

for Joel & Laura

This winter equinox is different from any other—
it's not the lizard men
playing ping-pong through the trees, the lighter-than-air
balls red with sunset; their sleeves
dressed with the feathers of dead Medici falcons.

A cow looks nervously at its eye
reflected in the ice
that the farmer breaks, releasing
the rope in the tree
and its black anvil weight falling...

The cow now looks at its eye
reflected in water,
thinking this is its cruel nativity—
the farmer looking at its lame hind leg
thinking of his red-haired brother-in-law,
the local butcher.

The sensitive cow, Mirtle, now charges the winter pond.
She drowns. The poor cow's tail
still flagging the spaceships just
behind the reddening hill.

So, the sun's down, the ship's lights
are like obvious fat jewels. And
if we want to have commerce
with the lizard men in their blue suits,
then we must eat more of these slouching animals
and faster too.

Gampopa's Gompa

Tibet, Dak Lha house… circa 1137 C.E.

The mountain cold annuls the dung brick.
The unwanted straw niche is plugged with black
volcanic mud, with leathery dead leeches, inches
long, brought up from berry fields

that sit beside the jaundiced glacier.
The howling wind is some dead sister in childbirth
or a secret choir of men in snow orbits
who know the winter is not troubled
by the skin of the salt field
it brings with it.

Two monks
struggle up the slope, the fat one
thinking of a weak warm beer, the other
of the large vulva of the storm

that moves in a strange
but secretly tropical compass
of imperfect songs
like the tongues of the young lovers
or the hurled inert calculations of an atom
gone wrong.

The Sentimentalists

The poet Apollinaire said something
memorable —
forgive my ignorance…
as I walk off to war,
never to be seen again.

He died on the night
of the Armistice. His head
wrapped in linen bandage —
his red-haired Russian mistress
calming him with a cooling vapor
off the prunebutter on cake
while below him on the street —
below her balcony
of ficus trees and small persimmons —

flocks of the dead rose
into the watercolorist's night sky,
dark wardens with magpie wings assisting…
battlefields drying of the blood,
feces, and bee paraffins by late spring.

Below her balcony, Parisians
passed like a river, crying
in one voice:
      Death to *Guillaume*, death
to *Guillaume* (the German Kaiser's name),

but Guillaume Apollinaire thought, under the knives
of a septic sinus and fever,
that all of Paris wanted this death;

so he died, there and then,
just to please the stupid sons-of-bitches.

Until then he was dying like a fence—
now, make no mistake—   it was
the end of all war as we knew it. And
please calculate the inchoate difference.
He was dying
like a fence. *Death to ignorance.*

Death to ignorance.

Goya

Rounds of bone and blood-rag scatter
from their backs
into the stacked hay.
The executions are endless—the men
die like nouns, with the weight of nouns.

The straw is a universe of brain and lung, lichen
and short stalk, lace and speckle wort.
The smell of the burnt powder
makes the experienced horses urinate in fear.
They lock and glide through mud, they shake.
They dance forward as if in a field
of snakes. Actually,

the lizard men walk by nervously till evening.
Then some charcoal and water
and the boys who moved whole schedules
of ammunition all day
get to sleep in the clean barn.

Again the stars begin to persecute me
like the crying cows in the next meadow
who have not been milked since Sunday.

Sky Harbor

The flock of pigeons rises over the roof,
and just beyond them, the shimmering asphalt fields
gather their dull-colored airliners.

It is the very early night,
a young brunette sits before the long
darkening glass of the airport's west wall.

She smells coffee burning
and something else—   her old mother's
bureau filled with mothballs.

Her nearly silver blouse smells of anise
and the heat of an iron.
She suddenly brushes sleep from her hair.

I have been dead for hours. The brunette
witness to nothing studies her new lipstick
smeared on a gray napkin.

The fires of a cremation tank are rising…
she descends into Seattle
nervous over the blinking city lights

that are climbing to meet her flight.
The old man seated next to her closes his book.
He has recognized her.

And leans into the window
to whisper, *nothing happens. Nothing
ever happens.*

For My Friend Sush Quintero,
Who Brought Me a Book

I

Who ever would occupy a ladder for very long?
Taking out the crystal loupe?
Does he eat an open sandwich? Is he
a prisoner of this quatrain? Is this inch of prose

his coffin? Has he concealed the diamond in his mouth?

There is a bone button there as well.
This poem is a result

of the dictations of sleep.

II

Mr. Edward Teller, father to our thermonuclear arsenal,
was troubled by the local desert
while a friend literally drove him down to the river
for an orange soda and a wrist corsage.

It was then that the flag-draped quatrain passed before them.
My excellent friend removing his straw hat. It was
like most coffins—
just five boards, especially the checkerboard,
two doors,
and two missing leafs from a boyhood table. *This must
be a burial in the river.* The courtyard

filling with crepe and long yellow peppers...

III

Nanzia had drowned in the Salt.
It was not the death she had dreamt of…

Begin agreeably by refusing some rounded or plump scotch—
this second pattern that refuses alcohol and smoke
feels good about itself but wouldn't
recognize, outside of these habits
of destruction, a major marble or the simple
kindness that says, "Mother, the pine woods
have cooled now that the storm has passed us—
wouldn't you rather nap now,
I will shell the beans for supper.

I've peeled the potatoes while listening to the radio.
They pulled the dead aunt from the river last night.
No, Mother, I don't believe there's anything to
this bird influenza
but I'll put some vinegar
in your bedside water.

There're rose hips in the tin.
Yes, the rivers flashed *there* and at Sunflower.
No, dear, I hadn't heard of drowning as an ecstatic death.

I would prefer to pass in my sleep
without a loose thread to my dream…

Yes, I suspect that some day everyone
on Earth will be ancient
like sea turtles or elephants. No beards
in summer, this time, Mother. Just hard science
and its superstitions.

I don't remember standing in snow, in Winslow,
and spelling both *ecstatic* and *elbow* for you?
Yes, how terrible to swallow a diamond
in the protocols of extinction. There was
some lightning with the storm. I'm glad
you missed that, yes, I think it does raise
gas in humans."

     IV.   *circa 1588...*
Elizabeth I loved a brilliant accounting
of a battle, with gusto and sea burials,
the coffin with a trapdoor,
H.M.S. CHECKERBOARD, the one box
used again and again—
no small savings to the Crown.
The ship's carpenter interrupts
with you can kiss my bloody cabbages. And we who
are about to die say,

you can kiss our cabbages. Mistress. Whore.

The linden shade along the river, a cadet
attempts to rap a green snapping turtle
on the snout with his long pole. Falls in
and drowns. The war ministers insist
on a formal burial on the river.
The turtles cleaning his bones in under a minute.

His mother's tears not yet done drying
on the patch of linen sail.
Xoas, Xoas, Xoas

        then, more waves.

V

If sitting on the sunbench, Mistress Anne
for the first time shifts Elizabeth
to the second breast, then Elizabeth and her Privy Council
of gangly men know this to be a prediction of future famine.

All this there in the infant who is jostled twice
then passed to a wet nurse and a further grim
exception to the feast of four breasts and, later,
six—it is said, nervously, that Anne Boleyn, had
a tertiary nipple near her armpit?

My god, but Elizabeth was civil
in her milk lessons—with her past
I would have gutted
Essex right there in the orchard of the first kiss.

But that's a man for you—clean,
functioning like memory itself.

And all liberty and faith
waits on the creeping vegetable state
of the state of the aging human mind.
It's nearly a joke about the still-operative memory
of the lover who is just now asked
to make of past pleasures,
a Cathay-fan accomplishment of fear…

I've not experienced
the above cancellations of mummery and inertia
while eating the harsh saltines of a Portuguese mescaline.
Yet it would force a fresh conclusion
regarding the teachings of our Lord Jesus.
He who insisted

that privilege is the adamantine ignorance—
that the black ants of the sprawling dirt of Bhopal, India,
are closer to the cosmic Christ
than Fat Wolsey with all his coins and vinegar spirits.

VI

I opened the book—will never forget
the small boy's face sewn back together
by a five-inch centipede, or baseball stitch,
and how he flinched under all that morphine
having had his face
separated there in the rain of Fallujah,

or the two sisters who were burned,
the skin now a tangerine bubble wrap.
Their eyes confused and innocent, as if to say
we will not ever be bad again.

There were these three girls standing
near a packet boat
near the outskirts of Hiroshima. The skin
on their arms, a poorly baked clay
with red grape leaf. Ashes on their eyelids.
The smaller of the three looked into me
there in the darkened Paramount Theatre.
I began to weep and a well-situated uncle
slapped me up against my shaved head. There was
an epidemic of ringworm
in all the barbershops
in and around the quarries—

the grown men let their hair grow
and we were shaved, acolytes
to a little pink circlet. It was springtime

and high-school girls were wearing
wrist corsages
because the necks of their colored gowns
had fallen nearly to the nipple line.

A young friend once stood in the polish of an auditorium
and said *everywhere, everything is feeding. And*
I'm still practicing a slight bow
and how to accent the "hello."

He closed his eyes while parachutes settled
down around him. The flak of flashbulbs intermittent

on his waxed forehead.

VII

There are women hanging wash, in China,
and they see a sick black dog eating its excrement
on the hillside.

Ezekiel is eating the diamond sandwich. He says,
You rich bastards
will love the iguana enema that is waiting for you
in wild fields of mustard and gorse...   wilder than
anything that landowner Bosch thought of...

but first we'll string colored lights
across the courtyard.
The Mariachi lift up their impossible instruments.
The people are sick.
We're asked not to congregate. It's really none
of your business.

Near the mound of hay, freshly turned,
a small boy pees into his dead aunt's mouth,
a dark field of rain turns toward the south.

Now her little Ezekiel kneels to steal the diamond
from her mouth, to steal
the pink gasoline corsage—   this quatrain, not yet finished,
must be her slow coffin, the river

her sad entourage…

On a Low Almond-shaped Mesa

elegy for Dorothy Lykes

The desert night carries heavy braids
of fresh salt to the river's thicket,
a brass wireless telegraph of locusts
talks to the busy
sand caves—   fruit bats
now arguing about the sun
that is just beyond the cold mountains.

You said you were
a small girl
when with effort
you unlocked the lacquered steamer trunk
filled with scraps of ermine,
"French tintypes,"
and the red box of talc—

but what you saw was a thousand-year-old
desert tortoise
journeying across a moon
of wild tan flowers.

You knew suddenly, you said,
why the dead were gathering
there in sand caves
at the very edge of a metropolis.

You were not exhausted,
you told
your daughter,

carrying your watering can
to young individual tea slips
in brick-colored pots, the sun
rising higher behind you
like yet another happy coincidence of thought.

George Herbert

We'd come back against the rain
looking for an old book of poems
I'd left on a red granite shelf
above a radiator
with wet rags of chalk, mostly
holidays and train schedules,
burning on it.

We'd been in the post office
shipping a manuscript to Estonia,
but noticed instead a green pen
and its long chain, the plastic stalk
chewed by a very nervous
animal only inches long—my daughter

thought we should name this naughty
toothy creature
still wild in a small village in Vermont…

I said, "Okay, George Herbert,"
she giggled, and the winter rain
lightened to snow
and our early supper, I remember,
was absolutely delicious.
Some whitefish with carrots.

Epithalamium

The sun dips in the neighbor's tall trees,
he has elevated his red rowboat
with stone blocks, the bats
cross once through the claustrophobic rain, he is calling
to the few horses of the old Evinrude motor…

In paper slippers
I am listening to the slow sledge
of an approaching heavy thunderhead.
I'm drinking coffee on the back step
while Jim in his orange canvas slicker
hopes to reach a few poor horses of gasoline,
a firing back across the empty lake,
some sudden soft generation like sleep.

At sixty, I love
a strange new woman with intensity,
and she loves me.
It's enough to make me believe
wholly in what turns
over, the neighbor calling, cranking
the black flywheel with a remnant of glacial
acrylic rope that he stole
from our rubbish can yesterday,
at dawn, just before two happy dogs
set it to rolling down this lovely green hill.

Poem in Praise of the Pacifist Abigail

In the old parsonage the parsnips
are blue, is
what I said to you. Parsnips
are pearl or white, quite,
if in clear sight, you argued.

Moose are blue in the pond—
are blue at noon—
is my warrant and song.

Moose are green in the evening
is my spleen and harmony.

In the volleying of sun and moon
moose are seen assailing their powdered beards,

and the taxi-ing loons fully adore them.
The good news is Abigail loves
everyone without reason.
She is my hero, my strange liaison.

A Midnight Star

is on the water. The winter moon
is there also
in its last quarter.

An empty wooden boat
collects them both.

What long mantle of snow
is over...

It is the year
of fires on the darkening shoulders
of Kilimanjaro.

Please, count your dollars.

A Practical Song of Two

for Hannah and Joel

Why not just being there, eye-level
across the water
in a precession of equinox, extract
of dark pericarp, of night—
in our own vast starless sleep
we are the tea-maker in the icehouse,
candle smoke
within falling escalators
of plaster and straw
transfused now with a marrow floor
of flowering rue.

All the doubtless new animals of summer
tossing like nets
their picnic blankets, preparations
for a county marriage, broken flare box,
sweet chutes of hail falling here and there,
my daughter,
into the meadows of Vermont.
Insects and telegraph lines
are humming to the light of no contract, private
yet as a miner in the Klondike
starved for weeks, ore
or wheat, fishing from the dock in rain with dynamite.

About the Author

Norman Dubie was born in Barre, Vermont, in April 1945. His poems have appeared in many magazines, including *American Poetry Review*, *Antaeus*, *The Paris Review*, *The New Yorker*, *Poetry*, *TriQuarterly*, and *Field*. He has won the Bess Hokin Award of the Modern Poetry Association and fellowships from the Ingram Merrill Foundation, the John Simon Guggenheim Memorial Foundation, and the National Endowment for the Arts. Mr. Dubie won the PEN USA prize for best poetry collection in 2001. He has recently published a book-length futurist work, *The Spirit Tablets at Goa Lake*, with *Blackbird*, the online magazine of *The New Virginia Review*. He lives in Tempe, Arizona, with the cat Fast-Eddy-Smoky-Chokyi-Lodrö, and teaches at Arizona State University.

Copper Canyon Press gratefully acknowledges
Lannan Foundation for supporting the publication and
distribution of exceptional literary works.

LANNAN LITERARY SELECTIONS 2007

Maram al-Massri, *A Red Cherry on a White-tiled Floor: Selected Poems*

Norman Dubie, *The Insomniac Liar of Topo*

Rebecca Seiferle, *Wild Tongue*

Christian Wiman, *Ambition and Survival: Becoming a Poet*

C.D. Wright, *One Big Self: An Investigation*

LANNAN LITERARY SELECTIONS 2000–2006

Marvin Bell, *Rampant*

Hayden Carruth, *Doctor Jazz*

Cyrus Cassells, *More Than Peace and Cypresses*

Madeline DeFrees, *Spectral Waves*

Norman Dubie, *The Mercy Seat: Collected & New Poems, 1967–2001*

Sascha Feinstein, *Misterioso*

James Galvin, *X: Poems*

Jim Harrison, *The Shape of the Journey: New and Collected Poems*

Hồ Xuân Hương, *Spring Essence: The Poetry of Hồ Xuân Hương,*
    translated by John Balaban

June Jordan, *Directed by Desire: The Collected Poems of June Jordan*

Maxine Kumin, *Always Beginning: Essays on a Life in Poetry*

Ben Lerner, *The Lichtenberg Figures*

Antonio Machado, *Border of a Dream: Selected Poems,*
    translated by Willis Barnstone

W.S. Merwin
    The First Four Books of Poems
    Migration: New & Selected Poems
    Present Company

LANNAN LITERARY SELECTIONS 2000–2006, CONTINUED

Taha Muhammad Ali, *So What: New & Selected Poems, 1971–2005,* translated by
Peter Cole, Yahya Hijazi, and Gabriel Levin

Pablo Neruda
The Separate Rose, translated by William O'Daly
Still Another Day, translated by William O'Daly

Cesare Pavese, *Disaffections: Complete Poems 1930–1950,*
translated by Geoffrey Brock

Antonio Porchia, *Voices,* translated by W.S. Merwin

Kenneth Rexroth, *The Complete Poems of Kenneth Rexroth*

Alberto Ríos
The Smallest Muscle in the Human Body
The Theater of Night

Theodore Roethke
On Poetry & Craft: Selected Prose of Theodore Roethke
Straw for the Fire: From the Notebooks of Theodore Roethke

Benjamin Alire Sáenz, *Dreaming the End of War*

Ann Stanford, *Holding Our Own: The Selected Poems of Ann Stanford*

Ruth Stone, *In the Next Galaxy*

Joseph Stroud, *Country of Light*

Rabindranath Tagore, *The Lover of God,* translated by Tony K. Stewart and
Chase Twichell

Reversible Monuments: Contemporary Mexican Poetry, edited by
Mónica de la Torre and Michael Wiegers

César Vallejo, *The Black Heralds,* translated by Rebecca Seiferle

Eleanor Rand Wilner, *The Girl with Bees in Her Hair*

C.D. Wright, *Steal Away: Selected and New Poems*

Matthew Zapruder, *The Pajamaist*

The Chinese character for poetry is made up of two parts: "word" and "temple." It also serves as pressmark for Copper Canyon Press.

Since 1972, Copper Canyon Press has fostered the work of emerging, established, and world-renowned poets for an expanding audience. The Press thrives with the generous patronage of readers, writers, booksellers, librarians, teachers, students, and funders—everyone who shares the belief that poetry is vital to language and living.

Major funding has been provided by:

Anonymous (2)

The Paul G. Allen Family Foundation

Beroz Ferrell & The Point, LLC

Lannan Foundation

National Endowment for the Arts

Cynthia Lovelace Sears and Frank Buxton

Washington State Arts Commission

THE **PAUL G. ALLEN** **FAMILY** *foundation*

NATIONAL ENDOWMENT FOR THE ARTS

WASHINGTON STATE ARTS COMMISSION

For information and catalogs:

COPPER CANYON PRESS
Post Office Box 271
Port Townsend, Washington 98368
360-385-4925
www.coppercanyonpress.org

The typeface is Janson Text, designed by Hungarian traveling scholar Miklós Kis in the 1680s. Display type set in Ellington, a font by contemporary master of letterforms in stone, metal, and ink, Michael Harvey. Book design and composition by Valerie Brewster, Scribe Typography. Printed on archival-quality Glattfelter Author's Text at McNaughton & Gunn, Inc.